PIANO • VOCAL • GUITAR

TOP CHRISTIAN HITS OF 2003-2004

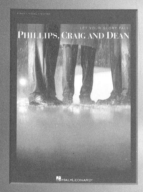

ISBN 0-634-07426-1

HAL•LEONARD® CORPORATION

7777 W. BLUEMOUND RD. P.O. BOX 13819 MILWAUKEE, WI 53213

Visit Hal Leonard Online at
www.halleonard.com

CONTENTS

ALL ABOUT LOVE

Words and Music by
STEVEN CURTIS CHAPMAN

We've got

DIFFERENT KIND OF FREE

Words and Music by LYNN NICHOLS,
ROBERT MARVIN, ALISA GIRARD,
CHRISSY CONWAY, KRISTIN SWINFORD
and MATT KEARNEY

Moderately

(Ah.) _____

1. Brok - en hearts, brok - en homes; there's a war deep in mo - tion.
2. Plead - ing the most worth - y cause for the in - no - cence we lost, __
3. *(See Rap lyrics)*

Fight - ing hard to __ find some kind of peace of __ mind. Breath - ing in, breath - ing out;
with His tears of __ blood, He start - ed free - dom's __ flood. As the world's o - pin - ions sway,

miss - ing life, liv - ing doubt. Search - ing for a __ cure, some kind of o - pen __ door.
my be - liefs will not be changed. Noth - ing ev - er __ can _____ take me from His __ hand.

16

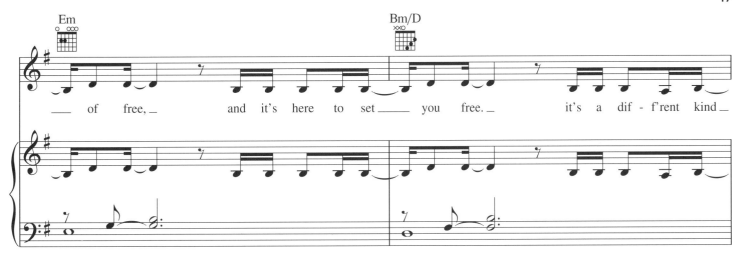

of free, ___ and it's here to set ___ you free. ___ it's a dif - f'rent kind ___

of free, ___ oh... _____

Rap Lyrics

Yeah, sure, I remember.
Matter of fact, it was just last September.
She still calls it "the fall to remember";
Little Heather, when it all came together.

Said, you remember the first time you met her?
She'd cry when it rains and blame the weather,
But inside she's strained with suicide letters,
The kind of cold you couldn't warm with a sweater.

Hardly lasted past December; she
Said she was headed down to defeat.
That's the last you'd seen, and never had dreamed
That the same little Heather, it's who you saw last week,

In an instant, you couldn't have missed her gleam.
As she listened, she looked like a distant queen.
With a difference, there for all to see,
She found a different, a different kind of free.
(To Chorus)

DIRTY

Words and Music by MARK STUART,
WILL McGINNISS, BOB HERDMAN,
TYLER BURKUM and BEN CISSELL

Moderately fast

Tired of be - ing clean, _ sick of be - ing _ prop - er. Wan - na live a - mong _ the beg - gars and

DO YA? DO YA?

Words and Music by
MICHELLE TUMES

Moderate Hip-Hop groove

Do ya like the freck - les on ___ my
Do ya like the way ___ I go ___ all

face? Do ya like my teeth? They're out ___ of place. ___ I like to think ___
shy? I just can't look ___ you in ___ the eye. ___ I like to think ___

EVERYTHING TO ME

Words and Music by CHAD CATES
and SUE SMITH

Male: I grew up ___ in Sun - day School; ___ I mem - o - rized the Gold - en Rule ___ and how

Je - sus came ___ to set the sin - ner free. ___ I

I want to tell __ the world __ I've found __ a

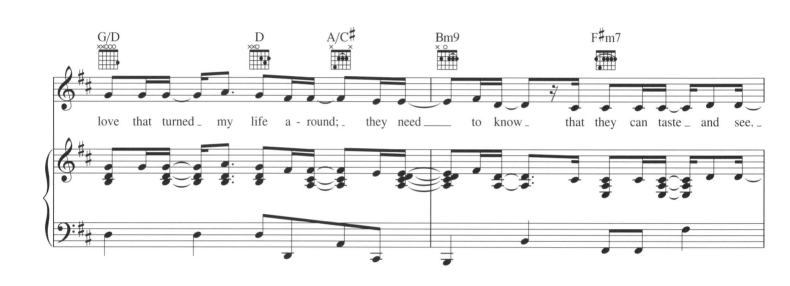

love that turned __ my life a - round; __ they need ____ to know __ that they can taste __ and see. __

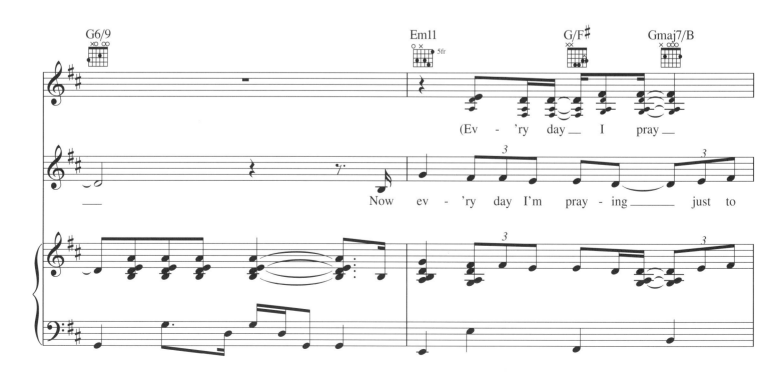

(Ev - 'ry day __ I pray __

Now ev - 'ry day I'm pray - ing _____ just to

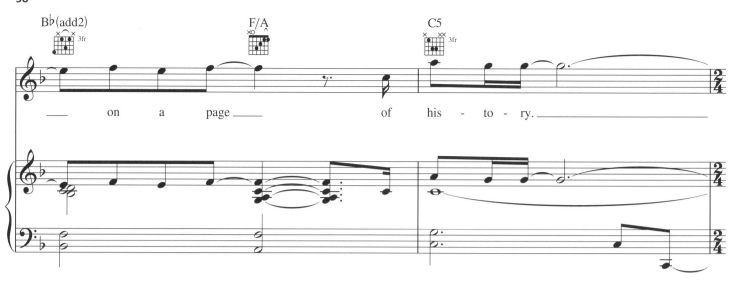

on a page _____ of his - to - ry. _____

(Ev - 'ry - thing ____ to me.) ____

Female: You're ev - 'ry - thing to me; You're
____ (Ev - 'ry - thing ____ to me, ____

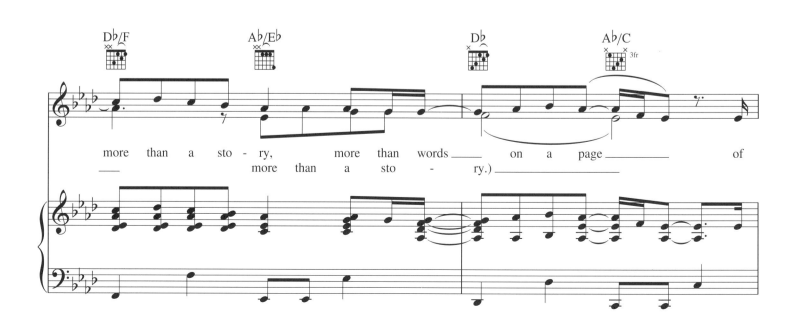

more than a sto - ry, more than words _____ on a page _____ of
____ more than a sto - ry.) _____

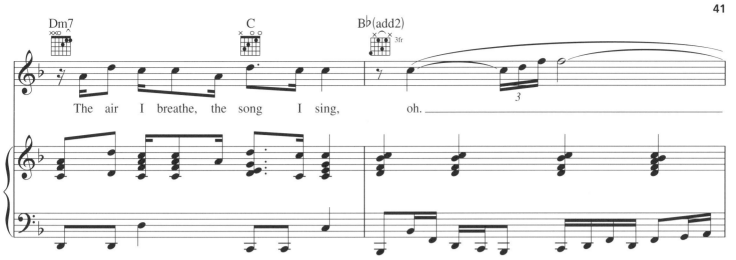

The air I breathe, the song I sing, oh. _____

____ (Ev - 'ry - thing ___ to me.) ___ (You're ev - 'ry - thing ___ to me, yeah.) ___ You're

(Ev - 'ry - thing ___ to me.) _____

my life ___ and my ev, ev - 'ry - thing. _____

GOD OF ALL

Words and Music by
TWILA PARIS

I CAN ONLY IMAGINE

Words and Music by
BART MILLARD

HOLY

Words and Music by NICHOLE NORDEMAN
and MARK HAMMOND

I STILL BELIEVE

Words and Music by
JEREMY CAMP

E - ven when I don't see, __

I still be - lieve. __

To Coda

72

I THANK YOU

Words and Music by REBECCA ST. JAMES,
MARC BYRD, LINDA ELIAS
and STEVE HINDALONG

IT IS YOU

Words and Music by
PETER FURLER

Moderately slow

As we lift up our hands, ___ will You meet us here? ___ As we call on Your name, _

___ will You meet us here? ___ We have come to this place ___ to wor - ship You, _

___ God of mer - cy and grace. ___ It is You ___ we a - dore. _

LEGACY

Words and Music by
NICHOLE NORDEMAN

I don't mind __ if you've __ got some-thing nice to say a-bout __ me, and I en-joy __ an ac-co-lade, like __ the rest, and you could take __ my pic-ture and hang it in __ a gal-ler-y of all the "who's __

MEANT TO LIVE

Words and Music by JONATHAN FOREMAN
and TIM FOREMAN

Fum - bl - ing __ his con - fi - dence __ and won - d'ring why the world __ has passed __ him by. _____

MORE LOVE, MORE POWER

Words and Music by
JUDE DEL HIERRO

MY PRAISE

Words and Music by DAN DEAN,
DAVE CLARK and DON KOCH

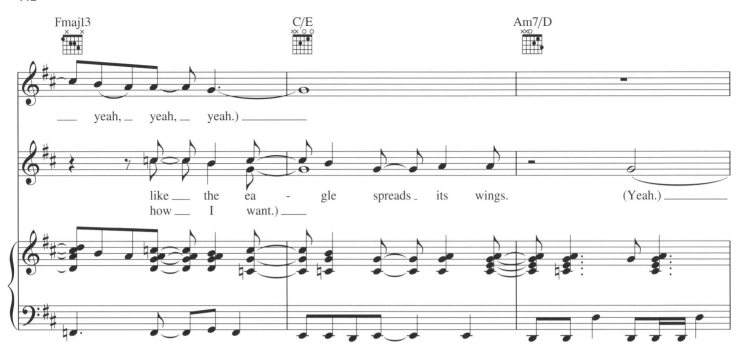

yeah, ___ yeah, ___ yeah.) _____

like ___ the ea - gle spreads ___ its wings. (Yeah.) _____
how ___ I want.) _____

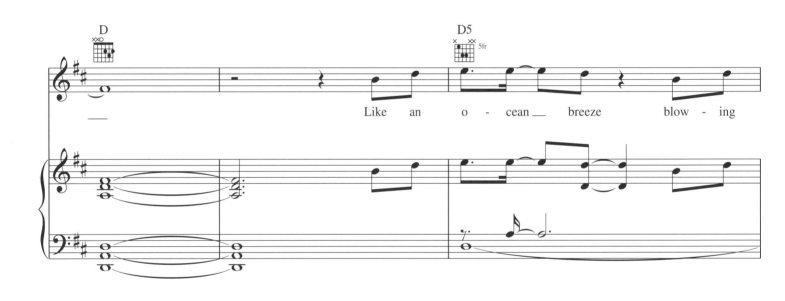

Like an o - cean ___ breeze blow - ing

on Your face, like a sum - mer ___ sun with its warm em - brace, like a

SAY IT LOUD

Words and Music by CHRIS ROHMAN
and MATT HAMMITT

It may be to - mor - row
And all of your rea - sons,

Original key: Db major. This edition has been transposed up one half-step to be more playable.

year.   year.

A twen-ty hour __ drive through the

Rock - y Moun - tains,   won't be stop - pin' now, 'cause you know we're rock - in'.

PRAY

Words and Music by DENNIS MATKOSKY,
KEITH BROWN and MARIA VIDAL

_____ my knees _ beg - gin' You, please, _ ev - 'ry time _ I stum - ble. Lord, _ I pray _

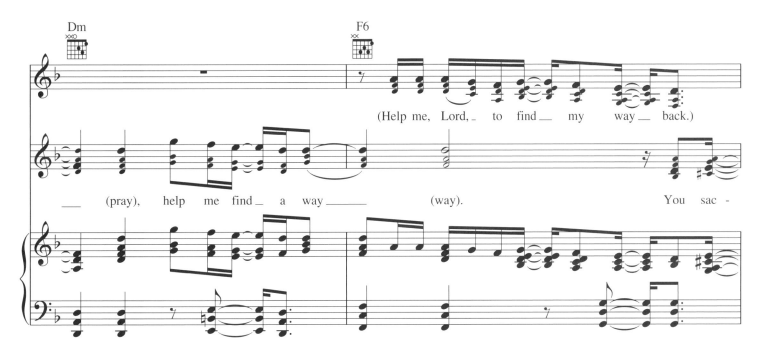

(Help me, Lord, _ to find _ my way _ back.)

_____ (pray), help me find _ a way _____ (way). You sac -

- ri - ficed, _ paid with _ Your life, _ gave me _____ the right. Lord, I pray. _

SHOW ME YOUR GLORY

Words and Music by MARC BYRD,
MAC POWELL, MARK LEE, BRAD AVERY,
TAI ANDERSON and DAVID CARR

STRONG ENOUGH

Words and Music by
STACIE ORRICO

Moderately slow

To Coda

YOU ARE SO GOOD TO ME

Words and Music by DON CHAFFER,
BEN PASLEY and ROBIN PASLEY

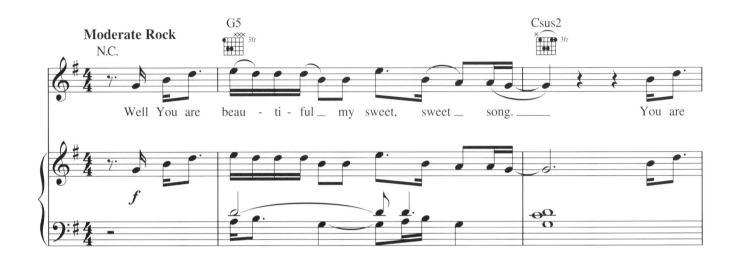

died up-on the cross. You are my Je - sus who loves

me. You poured out all Your blood. You died

up-on the cross. You are my Je - sus who loves

D.S. al Coda
(take 2nd ending)

me, yeah. You are

CODA

and I will sing a - gain. You are

YOU GET ME

Words and Music by CHRISSY CONWAY
and JAMES KATINA

THE CHRISTIAN MUSICIAN

THE CHRISTIAN MUSICIAN series celebrates the many styles of music that make up the Christian faith. From Gospel favorites to today's hottest Christian artists, these books have something for all Christian musicians! There is no song duplication between any of the books!

CHRISTIAN ROCK

30 songs from today's hottest Contemporary Christian artists, including Audio Adrenaline, DC Talk, Delirious?, FFH, Jennifer Knapp, Jars of Clay, and Newsboys. Songs include: Consume Me • Everything • Flood • Get Down • Joy • One of These Days • Shine • Undo Me • and more.
00310953 Piano/Vocal/Guitar............$16.95

CLASSIC CONTEMPORARY CHRISTIAN

30 favorites essential to all Christian music repertoire, including: Arise, My Love • Awesome God • Friends • The Great Divide • His Strength Is Perfect • Love in Any Language • People Need the Lord • Where There Is Faith • and more.
00310954 Piano/Vocal/Guitar............$14.95

CLASSIC PRAISE & WORSHIP

Over 30 standards of the Praise & Worship movement, including: As the Deer • Great Is the Lord • He Is Exalted • Lord, I Lift Your Name on High • More Precious Than Silver • Oh Lord, You're Beautiful • Shine, Jesus, Shine • Step by Step • and more.
00310955 Piano/Vocal/Guitar............$14.95

CONTEMPORARY CHRISTIAN HITS

30 of today's top Christian favorites, from artists such as Avalon, Steven Curtis Chapman, DC Talk, MercyMe, Nichole Nordeman, Point of Grace, Rebecca St. James, ZOEgirl, and others. Songs include: Always Have, Always Will • Between You and Me • Can't Live a Day • Dive • Fool for You • God Is God • I Can Only Imagine • If This World • If You Want Me To • A Little More • Live Out Loud • My Will • Run to You • Steady On • Testify to Love • Wait for Me • and more.
00310952 Piano/Vocal/Guitar............$16.95

COUNTRY GOSPEL

Over 40 favorites, including: Church in the Wildwood • Crying in the Chapel • I Saw the Light • I Wouldn't Take Nothing for My Journey Now • Put Your Hand in the Hand • Turn Your Radio On • Will the Circle Be Unbroken • Wings of a Dove • and more.
00310961 Piano/Vocal/Guitar............$14.95

GOSPEL'S FINEST

Over 40 Gospel greats, including: Because He Lives • The Day He Wore My Crown • Great Is Thy Faithfulness • How Great Thou Art • In the Garden • More Than Wonderful • Precious Lord, Take My Hand • Soon and Very Soon • There's Something About That Name • and more.
00310959 Piano/Vocal/Guitar............$14.95

MODERN WORSHIP

Over 30 popular favorites of contemporary congregations, including: Above All • Ancient of Days • Breathe • The Heart of Worship • I Could Sing of Your Love Forever • It Is You • The Potter's Hand • Shout to the Lord • You Are My King (Amazing Love) • and more.
00310957 Piano/Vocal/Guitar............$14.95

SONGS FOR A CHRISTIAN WEDDING

35 songs suitable for services or receptions, including: Answered Prayer • Celebrate You • Doubly Good to You • Faithful Friend • Go There with You • Household of Faith • I Will Be Here • If You Could See What I See • My Place Is with You • Parent's Prayer (Let Go of Two) • Shine on Us • 'Til the End of Time • Where There Is Love • and more.
00310960 Piano/Vocal/Guitar............$16.95

SONGS OF FAITH FOR KIDS

50 favorites for kids of all ages! Includes: Arky, Arky • The B-I-B-L-E • Down in My Heart • God Is Bigger • He's Got the Whole World in His Hands • He's Still Workin' on Me • I'm in the Lord's Army • Lord, Be Glorified • Jesus Loves the Little Children • Salt and Light • This Little Light of Mine • Zacchaeus • and more.
00310958 Piano/Vocal/Guitar............$14.95

FOR MORE INFORMATION,
SEE YOUR LOCAL MUSIC DEALER,
OR WRITE TO:

HAL•LEONARD®
CORPORATION
7777 W. BLUEMOUND RD. P.O. BOX 13819
MILWAUKEE, WISCONSIN 53213

Visit Hal Leonard Online at
www.halleonard.com

Prices, contents, and availability subject to change without notice.